# The \

MW01681173

Rob Halliburton

ISBN: 978-1-80128-866-8

# Dedication

To my beloved late mother and father, despite them not being physically present, the thought of them kept me strong throughout the entire experience of being paralyzed. I love them dearly, and I miss them every second. I aim to make them proud.

# Acknowledgments

I'd like to give a special thanks to Seth and Amy for being instrumental in the support that helped me carve my path. They graciously assisted me with the YouTube video. They ensured they visited me while I was in rehab to offer me support.

I'd also like to thank Patricia Dillion, who took great care of me. I would like to thank Carolyn Anderson, since she had an entire team of people who would keep praying for my recovery and well-being.

I'd like to thank my sister, Monica, who is my heartbeat and soldier. I don't know if I could've made it without her. She kept me motivated throughout my journey.

I'd also like to thank Poway Health Care Center, none of this would have been possible without them.

I'd also extend my gratitude to Collins Ghostwriting, the whole team of writers and support, who took my journey as their own and helped bring my story to life.

Lastly, I'd like to offer special thanks to Damon Robinson Sr., my brother-in-law, who was there from the very beginning and has been on my team the whole time.

# Contents

# About the Author

Rob Halliburton is a well-known public speaker who has also dedicated himself to the church as an ordained minister and evangelist. He has been known for speaking about his life story to motivate others and serve God, who blessed him with a miracle.

As an adolescent, Rob was an ace basketball player and would regularly play with his team in high school. His outstanding performance in basketball ended up landing him a scholarship in college.

Later in life, Rob decided to explore other opportunities that would allow him to grow and secure a stable career. Rob worked as a sales professional before starting his career as a bounty hunter and investigator. This profession ignited a passion in him, and he continued offering his services for the next two decades. During that period, he recruited and trained many bounty hunters, passing on the experience and expertise he gained throughout his service.

Rob has always dedicated himself to his fitness and actively participated in mountain bike races. He continued to do so until he met a tragic incident that left him paralyzed from the neck down. His trials during the heart-rending ordeal led him to connect to God, and he decided to chronicle his life story to give people a reason to keep fighting to live.

# Preface

For a long time, I thought I had a fair understanding of how the world worked and how people functioned. I was born to parents who dedicated everything they had to improve their children's lives. They were my heroes, and I wanted to be like them when I grew up.

I have always been an athletic person. I was an ace at sports in both high school and college. My passion continued to be a big part of any kind of sport I took up. I even began racing mountain bikes and participated in many races throughout my life. People used to be amazed at my emphasis on fitness as I remained vigorously energetic and active through my middle age.

Everything seemed to appear perfectly fine. My bounty-hunting career took up the span of two decades, and during this time, I had two children at home growing up like speeding bullets. It was the moment when I least expected a tragedy to strike that I was met with a grave fate.

In a matter of hours, the course of my life had altered. The man who used to run miles could no longer walk. The people who claimed to love and support me had left me to die. I had no one but God to guide me through the darkness. I was let down by none other than the person I trusted. It was the family that betrayed me, and I was left helpless.

After a long time of fighting the odds, contemplating my

relationships, and reconnecting with God, I finally decided to reveal my story to the people who have been struggling. And with it, I intend to ignite a flicker of hope that will enable people to regain their faith in life and God with this book.

# Chapter 1: The Beginning of the Torment

I like to believe I have lived two lives, one before the tragedy and one after it. I will describe what happened to me later, but I want to start with the life I was fortunate enough to have before everything went downhill.

Imagine a perfectly healthy man leading a normal life. I don't mean mediocre when I say normal. It was normal in the sense that I had almost everything one could ask for. I was fine with who I was. I would go out, I had friends I loved, and my family was also good to me.

I was born in East Chicago, Indiana, which is right outside of Chicago. I was the fifth of nine siblings. We were one big family, but we eventually moved out and went to different places.

Sports were always my passion, and I was a dedicated athlete. My performance in basketball ended up landing me a sports scholarship in college. It was a great start to the next chapter of my life. I didn't stick to one profession throughout my life as I have always believed in exploring new opportunities.

I worked as a bounty hunter and investigator nationwide for almost two decades. During this period of my occupation, I recruited and trained bounty hunters. I also happened to work as a sales professional for a while before becoming a well-known public speaker. I have been dedicated to my service to the church and served as an ordained minister and evangelist.

I was raised in a household led by two parents who single-handedly raised nine children in the projects in East Chicago, Indiana. My parents were never wealthy, yet they made sure that we had everything we needed while growing up.

The neighborhood I grew up in, the 219, carries many memories for me to this day. Everyone there struggled to make ends meet but ensured that a community was there to support them. It was a tough neighborhood to live in, but that didn't change the fact that it was the best place I had ever lived. I will always remember that neighborhood as the place that gave me many best friends who remain close to me even today.

My parents were a source of inspiration for me when I was going through the darkest times of my life. Those people served as heroes for me and taught me everything that I know today.

Unfortunately, they aren't alive anymore, but they left a great impact on my life. They were all I thought about whenever I came across a challenging situation in my life. I would always wonder what they would do in that situation.

I had two best friends, and they were my parents. They didn't teach me to quit, and no one knew me better than them. They were incredibly smart people who always put their children first before anyone. My father, Larthelle Halliburton, and mother, Lela Halliburton, will always remain the people I could turn to whenever I was distressed.

*My mother*

*My father*

I used to be fitter than most people my age. I used to be a mountain biker, and I was good at it. I even participated in a mountain bike marathon, so I had to be fit to do that. I was very healthy in that sense. I would even say that I still had my high school body. Not many people my age could say that.

I wasn't a couch potato. I liked to go out, meet people, and mingle. Sitting at home or office was not my thing. I liked being on the move, whether it was going out to get the groceries, running errands, or driving my friends somewhere. Of course, I had many friends who I liked to hang out with.

My parents had a huge family. They had nine kids, and I was number five among my siblings. You can say I was a middle child.

I have been a family man. I'm definitely not the person who would rarely see his mom and the rest of his family. I liked getting involved with family affairs. I never understood people who would choose to stay distant from their families.

That was never me.

If there was something going on, I had to know exactly what was happening. So I didn't act indifferent to the problems around me. I tried my best to help the people who needed me.

I have two kids, Rob and Robyn. They have always been my reason to wake up every day and live life to the fullest. I taught my kids the same love that my mother taught me. I would make sure that they wouldn't hurt anyone. I wanted them to be strong, but I also wanted them to have the ability to think twice before saying or doing anything. I knew the magnitude of influence words could have on people.

I can say that I am a sensitive person, and I don't think sensitivity is a sign of weakness. It's a strength. The strength to acknowledge what you have done is to think from someone else's perspective and feel what they feel like.

I have never been an understated person. I spoke what I wanted to speak, lived like I wanted to live, and felt what I felt. There was never any holding back from my end. Safe to say, I expected, if not the same, then the same degree of receptivity from people as well. I knew people wouldn't live up to my expectations. I mean, when did they ever do that? But I still didn't expect what the people I thought loved me would do.

I think about my late father often. He was a good person. He exemplified strength and patience. The virtues he taught me had served me well so far. He was a cool father and liked to stay close to his family. Maybe I inherited my life choices from him, and I hope my kids also did the same.

My sister Debra has had a big role in my life. She had a lot to do with what was to follow after a drinking night at her place. It was one of the normal days in Fresno. The weather was fine, and I wanted to go to my sister's place, so I did that.

Debra and I were close, or at least I thought we were. I cared for her as I cared for everyone else. But I believe she didn't feel the same way about me. She would be nice to me when she wanted to be. Debra was older than me; I think she was around three years older. Her family, including her husband, Damon, and her kids, were the only family I had on the West Coast.

I lived in San Diego, which is about 10 hours away from Fresno. I used to try to visit them as often as I could. We would stay near her place in a hotel and would hang out with the family.

Then came the day when everything was about to change. I was a 55-year-old man who had been living a healthy life. Little did I know that my life would turn upside down when I made the trip to Fresno.

We reached Debra's house. I was hoping for a relaxed evening. I had been very tired from all the work and dealing with the kids. My sister's house was a nice place to unwind. I didn't eat before going out because we would eat at hers.

We had our dinner, and then we went to the room where we usually used to sit and drink. Everything seemed fine. We talked about our day and how it was going for her. Then, I started talking about the kids. I talked about my kids a lot; they were a big part of my life. I don't think any parent ever stops talking about their kids because it's their full-time job.

We had a few things going on in the family, and we didn't get to talk more about the recent happenings because of the distance. We talked about our family and parents. I was super close to my mother, and she used to tell me about everything, but Debra used to have something to add to everything we talked about.

She had interesting information, hidden easter eggs, and some controversial opinions as well. Debra wasn't a boring person; she was interesting, but she would never say it all. She held back whatever she didn't want to be disclosed.

It was getting a little later, we were done with the food, and I finally had space in my stomach to have some liquor in my system. This was supposed to be the good part of the night. I was too tired to make the drinks, so I just sat back and waited for Debra to get up and make us drinks.

It took Debra a while to return with the drinks, but I asked her what had taken her so long when she finally returned. Debra began to pour a drink for me. Debra liked to drink beer as it was her drink; that was what she was drinking that night as well. I didn't notice that she hadn't poured one for herself. Instead, she told me she would pour herself one a little later. I thought maybe she was too tired and would drink when she felt more like it.

I started drinking, and we continued talking. Debra looked different that night. She wasn't in a cheerful mood, and she even looked slightly pissed at me at some point. Debra and I didn't always agree on everything.

We had different opinions, and we held our ground. Sometimes she would even get pissed at me, which was normal. I thought it was one of those times.

After I had a drink, I started feeling a sharp ache in my back. I thought it would go away, but it didn't. I tried moving, but I couldn't. That's when I started to get worried. Whenever I had a strain or something, I would stretch or move my body, and it used to work. I had no idea why it wasn't working this time.

My pain got intense real quick and to the point that I couldn't move at all. My entire body was in excruciating pain. I felt helpless and miserable. I started yelling, and Debra rushed to see what was happening.

It felt like I had a knot in the back, preventing me from moving. My body was shutting down. Debra started asking me where the pain was and if I could move. I told her that it was terrible and I was terrified. She didn't panic and tried to figure out what to do next.

I had no idea what was happening to me. I was completely fine a moment before, and now I couldn't move. I couldn't believe what was happening.

Was I having a stroke, or was it the end?

I had no idea whether I was going to make it. The world had stopped, and everything was limited to the pain I was having.

# Chapter 2: Suspicion of Betrayal

I was in immense pain when the paramedics arrived at my sister's place. I was in absolute misery, but they weren't gentle with me. Instead, they grabbed me aggressively and threw me in the back of the ambulance.

When I was lying on the stretcher in the vehicle, I noticed that the paramedic guy was talking to my sister on his phone. He was yelling at my sister, and they seemed to be arguing.

It was bizarre because why would he yell at my sister, and why were they arguing?

It seemed to like they knew each other.

Something was strange about the entire scene.

It was bizarre because why would he yell at my sister, and why were they arguing?

It seemed like they knew each other. I kept hearing them argue while lying on a stretcher in a paramedic van.

I was in immense pain, but my brain was working fine. I could see and hear everything around me. However, the ongoing situation made me anxious and added to the pain.

Why were my sister and this paramedic guy she called arguing?

My sister had just called for help, and she hadn't told me anything about knowing the person who came to my sister's house to take me to the hospital.

Debra would have mentioned it if she wanted me to know. Whatever she was doing was fairly suspicious, and I had every reason to doubt her intentions.

In retrospect, my sister could have suspicious intentions as I was totally fine one minute, and then I wasn't. In addition to all this, I was now being taken to a hospital by someone who apparently had known my sister before arriving at her house.

On top of everything, I was constantly watching them argue, and I couldn't understand why they were arguing exactly.

Was something wrong?

I might not have lived in Fresno, but I knew the place very well since my sister lived there, and I often visited her. So at least I knew the place well enough to know which hospitals were reliable. So I wasn't clueless in that sense.

I had heard about this reputable hospital in Fresno from people I knew there. I hadn't heard any complaints, and the people I knew preferred that place. People were treated well at the hospital; at least, it's what I had been hearing for a while.

I knew about the torment I was dealing with because it wasn't something that had just happened out of the blue. I was a healthy person and not just that. I was physically fit; then why me?

There was absolutely nothing wrong with my health, so what changed?

It wasn't a heart attack, hemorrhage, or any kind of stroke.

It was merely a knot in my back, so how was it hurting so bad?

I could have seen this coming in a million years.

A healthy person paralyzed because of a knot?

I couldn't believe it, but I was living it and suffering from it.

I wanted to make sure I was put out of this misery. Everything seemed strange: the paramedic guy knowing my sister and their argument made me more suspicious by the minute.

I wanted to be taken to a good hospital so they could figure out what was happening to me. I had heard all kinds of stories about mistreatment in hospitals, so I wanted to make sure that I was in safe hands.

I asked the paramedic guy to take me to a reputable hospital in Fresno, California. I was very certain about the hospital and hoped it would diagnose me properly. After all, an accurate diagnosis is the most important aspect of treating someone. I just didn't want to be mistreated. My life was too precious for me.

It was then up to the paramedic guy to take me to the hospital. However, even though I had made my choice very clear and insisted on going to that hospital, he ignored me.

What followed was just the beginning of the nightmare I was about to witness.

My sister intervened in the matter and started asserting that I needed to be taken to another hospital. Of course, anyone would have thought that she must be looking out for me and wanted me to be taken to an even better hospital. Well, that didn't happen.

To my shock, my sister wanted to take me to the ghetto hospital. There was this hospital in Fresno of ill repute for its poor service, functions, and more. It was known as a ghetto hospital. You can imagine by the sound of its nickname that it wasn't called that because it was good. The ghetto hospital was situated downtown, and it would have taken some time to get there.

I was very confused by all this.

Why would my sister suggest we go there instead of going to a reputable hospital?

Why was she opting for the opposite of my recommendation?

I was in immense pain, and we had no idea what was happening. My condition required a reputable and experienced doctor who could treat patients who showed up like me.

I had nothing in my control. I couldn't control the pain, misery, and anxiety my sister was causing me in such a severe condition. I was lying there without any control left over my life.

I had absolutely no say in a matter that solely involved me.

I was the one in pain, but Debra was dictating what should be done next.

How could she seize control of my life when I was being put through misery?

Debra kept insisting on taking me to the ghetto hospital. It was clear that she was in charge, and she was in control of my fate now. The paramedic guy did exactly what she said. It was decided that I would be taken to a hospital known as the ghetto.

My fate was decided there, in the paramedic vehicle by my sister. I was certain that I was going to die.

I was enraged and furious about my sister's behavior. I couldn't believe that my sister was doing this to me.

I decided not to give up.

I started to argue with her and yelled at the paramedic guy. If Debra could have been stubborn, so could I.

I kept yelling and asking the paramedic guy to take me to the hospital I wanted, not the one that my sister was telling him about. I wasn't going to make it so easy for her to take charge of my life because I had been robbed of my physical strength.

The yelling and argument continued. Debra would keep responding, emphasizing taking me to the ghetto hospital while I wouldn't budge a bit. I might have been physically unable to fight, but I was using all the strength I was left with to fight for my life.

My life didn't belong to my sister or the paramedic guy. It belonged to me.

They weren't the ones in intense pain; it was me.

So why would I let my sister, who wasn't even close to me, and this strange paramedic guy decide my fate? I refused to give up.

Debra was sure that she had control of my life now, but I wasn't standing down. I kept yelling, and she would also yell back. I was hell-bent on being taken to the hospital I wanted so my life could have been saved.

Among all the fighting and yelling, it felt like Debra didn't even intend to save my life. She was putting my life in danger. Yet, she was not backing down and was persistent with her whatever she wanted to do.

I remember everything perfectly well. I kept yelling at him to take me to a better hospital, but my sister insisted on going to the ghetto hospital. She didn't care about my request because she had decided what she wanted to do.

Debra had the last say, and of course, she won.

She was perfectly healthy, and I was lying on the stretcher. She had won custody of what happened next in my life.

The paramedic guy ended up taking me to the ghetto hospital.

I knew something extremely shady about my sister and the paramedic guy deciding to take me to the ghetto hospital. I had a sense of what was happening. They had taken on the authority to decide how I should be treated and, more importantly, where.

As I saw my life's control getting seized, I tried to take in everything around me: Debra, the paramedic guy, the vehicle, the road, and Village Glen. Everything seemed to be happening in a strange way. It felt like I was a spectator in my own life where I could only watch and not decide what happened next.

Everything started flashing in front of my eyes. One moment I was visiting my sister at her house and having a drink, and the next moment I was in the paramedic vehicle.

I can remember everything perfectly now. Everything from the glass to the vehicle is now imprinted in my brain. I remember sitting on a couch, the knot that I felt in my back, how my body stopped functioning, and the way that paramedic guy arrived.

The paramedic's vehicle stopped. Finally, we arrived where Debra wanted me. I was about to enter the ghetto hospital, and my fate would be decided in a while.

The paramedic people took me out of the vehicle as I was lying on a stretcher. I was in so much pain that I didn't even know if I would make it. I was finally taken to the hospital.

I entered the hospital, and suddenly I felt a sharpness in my body as if someone had stabbed me. I looked at the paramedic guy, and I saw a needle in his hand. It was a big needle and scary as well. I was shocked to see the needle inside my body. It was very painful.

I didn't understand why I was getting injected by this guy when I was about to meet a doctor in the hospital who would have taken a look at me and would decide what should be done with me.

The injection was so strong that I immediately felt its effect as everything started getting blurred. After that, I stopped seeing everything around me clearly. My vision was so blurred I could hardly make out who was in front of me.

It took me only seconds to realize that I was passing out. The injection wasn't meant to relieve my pain. It was meant to put me to sleep, so I couldn't see what was happening.

The last thing I saw before my world went dark was a sign of an emergency. My eyes were blinking. My surroundings seemed to be disappearing as my eyes closed.

I finally passed out.

When I now think about my life before this incident, I think about a healthy man with kids still participating in triathlons. Of course, no one of my age was doing that, but I was.

I was very confident about my physical fitness and how I carried myself. It was important to me to take care of my fitness as, at one point, you need to make an effort to take care of your body as it won't function as the body of a 20-something person.

People around me envied how fit I was, and I liked the attention. After all, I had worked hard for this. However, it's not easy to get up in the morning and decide that you're not going to be a lazy person.

Every day I chose to be physically active and engaged in activities that even young people wouldn't. For example, I have always liked mountain bike racing. I used to be so fascinated by these races that I also wanted to be a part of them one day.

Mountain bike racing requires a lot of strength as there is a great deal of risk involved with the marathon. The mountain is, of course, an extremely uneven and dangerous place.

It was hard enough to walk in those mountains, let alone ride my bike through them. Call it a thrill or an adrenaline rush. I liked whatever it was. I was physically fit enough to participate in it, so why not?

While I was participating in the mountain bike marathon, I realized how fortunate I was to be able to take part in something normal people wouldn't even dare to.

When I compare my life with the life I was about to have; it was an absolute nightmare. It was impossible for someone like me to imagine being stuck on a stretcher.

When I used to race through those rocky mountains, I felt like I had control over my life, and now that I couldn't even move, I saw that control getting robbed of me by someone biologically related to me.

The mountains had nothing on me, but this knot in my back had taken over all the control I had over my body. The pain extended to the rest of my body, and it started shutting down. I felt hopeless and still, rotting in pain, unable to figure out what was wrong with me.

How was it even fair for something so painful to happen to someone like me?

Imagine a mountain bike racer who was never afraid of anything in life and was now in a hospital bed. I had complete control over what happened in my life as I rode my bike, and now it felt like it was someone else who had that control over my life.

It was too much to take in. I think about everything that happens, and I often wonder how someone else would feel about a situation like that if they didn't have a life as I did.

Would it have been easier for someone other than me? Was it so hard on me because I had so much faith in myself and what my body could do?

The body that people envied was now depending on people in white coats and, of course, my sister. My strength was being taken away from me because of a mere knot in my back.

It's ironic how those rocky mountains couldn't mess with me, but this knot in my back was now ruining my life. My entire life was on the verge of ending on such a miserable note just because of a knot.

It couldn't have been true. There was more to it, and something was very wrong.

How could this knot in my back have been the most painful moment in my life?

I was strong, or at least I thought I was. I could have thought about what could hurt me, but this pain was never one of them. That is what was so infuriating. This pain made me question my entire life.

# Chapter 3: Almost Dead

People have preconceived notions about the end of their lives and what will happen when they die. Some believe death is merely a passage to the other world. Those who don't believe in the afterlife think about death as a switch; once it is turned off, you immediately stop existing.

For me, having a near-death experience was similar to death itself.

As soon as I closed my eyes, the entire world surrounding me stopped existing. I was alive, but I was unconscious. I had no idea where I was or whether I was alive or not. The real world had turned dark for me, and I had stopped existing in that world.

I was somewhere else, but I didn't recognize the place I was in. The place was somewhere in between life and death. It was not over, but I had entered a place where I had to fight for my life, and it was horrible.

I kept having terrifying nightmares when I was unconscious. Those nightmares weren't the normal ones anyone would have. It was excruciating, brutal, and disturbing. I was never peacefully sleeping or having nice dreams.

It was a constant trail of horrible nightmares that would never end. My mind would jump from nightmare to nightmare, and I could not do anything.

I can clearly remember that I had one nightmare about Debra. She appeared in my dream as this suspicious evil person with not-so-good intentions. Yes, it was my sister, but my subconscious thought that she might have been the culprit behind my situation.

Debra had evil intentions in my nightmares. She didn't seem to like me or show mercy. She was plotting something that would end up hurting me.

She was planning my ruin.

It all seemed too real not to believe, as if I had a spiritual delivery of a message from God about the person behind everything.

When I was in a coma, I had no idea how long I'd been in since I had been unconscious. I had been living in countless disasters and chaos while having nightmares. Hours turned into days, and days turned into weeks, and I was still unconscious with no sign of recovery.

I started hearing people one day.

It was all too blurry to make out or hear them properly. I heard doctors talking about some surgery. I thought I was still in that nightmare, but I wasn't. I was semi-awake, and I could listen to those voices. I was trying hard to listen to what they were saying.

After two weeks, I opened my eyes for the first time. It took me a while to come back to the real world. I had been in horrible pain ever since I had the incident. The last thing I remembered was the emergency sign of the room where I was being taken. I tried to think about what had happened and remembered the incident.

I saw a very different world when I woke up. I was in a hospital bed; all these machines were in the room: some were tracking my pulse and some my blood pressure. I had canolas inserted into my hands. I was not clothed as I could remember. I had picked the clothes myself and wore them before going to Debra's house, but these weren't the clothes I had worn before I came to the hospital.

The pain.

It suddenly hit me that I couldn't feel the excruciating pain.

I couldn't feel anything at all.

I recalled the incident and how bad the pain was. It was so horrible I felt like I was dying. I thought I was dead all this while, but I was, brought back to the real world in a blink of an eye.

Something wasn't right, and I could feel it in my heart. I tried to look at myself, but I was lying down, so it wasn't easy to see what was happening. I had been in a hospital, so I must have had a procedure or something. I needed to see if anything was done to my body because, for some reason, I couldn't feel anything at all.

It was heartbreaking to discover that I was paralyzed from the neck down.

How could it be possible?

I was a healthy and always on-the-go person, and here I was, limited to a hospital bed. One night changed my life, and I couldn't help it. People used to gush about how physically fit I was. I was doing so well.

I was happy, and I had a family.

Now, I was in that hospital bed alone, and I couldn't feel my legs, hands, or feet. It felt like I didn't even have anybody. The only part of my body I could feel was my face. But I couldn't lift my hand or walk on my feet.

The feeling of going from a healthy life to being confined to a hospital was horrible. I couldn't believe that it was happening. I was numb from the neck down, and there was no sensation. No matter what I tried, I couldn't move my legs or hands. It appeared as if they didn't even exist anymore. My body was there, but it wasn't working anymore.

God didn't leave my side when I felt the loneliest in my darkest times. I believe the determination I had to fight back and make it was driven toward me by God himself. I wasn't alone as long as he was with me.

I was under the protection of God, who was watching over me. That's when I realized that God is with those left on their own. When you don't have anyone standing by your side, God is.

When I was starting to wake up, people were talking to each other. I couldn't just open my eyes at once, it was taking a lot of effort to see what was happening around me, but I was aware of the surroundings. I think I was semi-awake, but not completely.

I heard someone talking about heart surgery, and it startled me. It felt like I was having another nightmare, a horrible feeling. They kept talking about surgery, and it made me anxious. I wanted to stop them, but I didn't have the energy to say something.

I had blurry vision, but I could somehow make out doctors and nurses wearing uniforms. They were constantly looking at me like I was some sort of object. Their eyes were trying to pierce my mind and notice every part of my body, but I couldn't see myself.

A heart surgery?

I was taken to the hospital for a backache, so why were these people talking about heart surgery?

My heart was perfectly fine, and I didn't need anyone to operate on me. I strongly felt that something very wrong was happening, and I had to do everything I could to stop it from happening.

Despite being in a coma, I was very well aware that I was taken to the hospital for backache and not a heart problem. I have always had a healthy heart. They might be attempting to do something that would harm me. I didn't trust those doctors at all. I didn't come to that hospital in the first place, and now that I was here, they were doing random procedures that could kill me.

I wanted to move my body, but I couldn't move. I was doing everything I could to move my body, but I was helpless. I was stuck in the hospital bed, and they were about to tear my heart open.

# Chapter 4: Fighting for My Life

Imagine losing control of your entire life.

Someone has taken over the steering wheel, and they turned it in a new direction. It's the last place you would want to be in, but you're stuck. You don't want to be here, and you're aware that you won't survive if you're taken to that place, but then again, you're stuck!

You can only scream and ask this person to spare you, but they won't.

No matter what you say, they won't listen to you.

You're being silenced.

You no longer have a voice and are just drifting now.

I didn't imagine all this.

It was my reality.

I was drifting while I was in a coma. I had no idea where I was, but I knew someone was trying to take my life from me. But I wasn't willing to go down without a fight. I might have been in a comatose state, but I was constantly fighting.

I refused to go away so easily as the person behind my misery thought I would.

I wasn't built like people my age.

I didn't play by the rules like others usually did.

I might have been chained to a hospital bed, but that didn't stop me from fighting for my life. I wasn't ready to be defeated. I could feel what was happening to me. They were trying to take over control of my life from me. Nobody wanted me to get better.

Instead, they were trying to make the situation worse. It appeared as if all the forces had aligned against me. I was the only one fighting for myself.

When I was in a coma, I was alone. I had no one to wake me up from those never-ending nightmares. It was just me, by myself, standing my ground to fight the demons. I couldn't tell reality from the nightmares, but whatever it was, I had to fight it.

I had to survive.

My nightmares were terrifying, but I was determined to fight them. I had to make it make to the real world.

The only thing that kept me going, even during my darkest times, was my belief in God. I didn't know where I was or if I would ever get out of it, but I knew I wasn't alone. If I was alone in the world, I wouldn't have been breathing.

I knew that God hadn't left me alone.

While I was in the coma, I felt God Himself protecting my spirit. Something inside was refusing to give up. I couldn't have gathered all that strength on my own. There was something else. A greater power was watching over me and ensuring I kept breathing.

As my body was left paralyzed and I couldn't move an inch, I sensed the presence of the Holy Ghost protecting my existence. No one might have physically guarded me, but that didn't mean God had given up on me.

He was still there.

He gave me the strength I needed to fight for my life. The doctors in the hospital I was staying in were incapable of treating me. I had been in a coma all this time, and it had all started with that sharp pain in my back. If only my sister had listened to me and taken me to a good hospital, I wouldn't have had to endure so much pain.

But that had been Debra's intention.

She didn't want me to survive in the first place. So here I was, stuck in an unknown hospital, surrounded by strangers, while the doctors treated me like their personal guinea pig.

This was no exaggeration on my part.

They had the authority to do whatever they thought was best for me.

They didn't care about my consent or my life.

I was treated like a piece in a museum. I wasn't a person anymore. The doctors would come in with their students, and I would be displayed in front of them.

They would ask me to move my arms which I couldn't. I was paralyzed, and I couldn't move at all. But they still asked me to move in front of the students. When they saw that I couldn't move, they didn't spare me any kindness and left me alone. Instead, they laughed at me as if I was an object solely purposed for their entertainment.

I still remember them asking me to move my arms like I was pushing someone. And all these faces saw me as incapable of controlling my own body. Their stupid blank faces turned into grinning. They didn't care that I was still alive and that whatever happened around me still affected me like it would affect anyone else.

I had never had a heart problem, but somehow the doctors at that hospital were convinced there was an issue with it and wanted to operate on my heart. There was no way I would have agreed with their diagnosis if I had full autonomy over myself. It was my life, and I should have had the last say in what happened to my body.

The doctors knew that my actual problem was my back since it was the root cause of my breakdown, which led me to this state. But they didn't do anything about it. I was paralyzed from the neck down because of my back. It didn't matter to them that I needed assistance with their back issues. Instead, they went for my heart, which was totally fine in the first place.

I was strictly against the heart surgery that the doctors wanted to perform on me. I had hardly survived the coma, and now they were preparing to put me into another life-threatening situation.

I didn't want to be sliced open against my wishes. But the doctors weren't willing to listen to me. I don't know if it was paranoia or instinct, but it seemed like they didn't want me to make it, just like my sister. So, I was trapped in a hell hole.

What surprised me more was that they weren't doing anything to help me heal from what I was suffering.

I didn't receive good treatment from that hospital.

In fact, the treatment was terrible. I wasn't getting better. I was constantly in pain, whether I was in a coma or when I found myself stuck to the bed, unable to move my body.

I can still remember the moments when I awoke from the coma. It was an unnerving moment when I started to wake up. Everything was so blurry, and I couldn't make out what was happening. I only heard the words that doctors were speaking.

Someone was talking about heart surgery, and suddenly it hit me that I was in a hospital and my heart was going to get operated on. It hit me that I would be sliced open if I didn't say anything.

I started yelling. My screams echoed in the hospital, and I was hysterical. I had just woken up from a dark place only to find out they were about to operate on my heart.

When the doctors saw that I had woken up, they were shocked. They couldn't believe that I had woken up. Perhaps, they had given up on me and thought I would not make it. But I fought to return to life and end all the nightmares.

I was finally conscious.

The doctors were only after my heart. They were so eager to operate on it as if it was extremely necessary. I didn't think it was important to cut open my heart. Instead, they could just try to diagnose what was actually wrong with my body and what exactly caused the pain that night.

Surprisingly, my sister told the doctors to go ahead and operate on my heart. It didn't matter to her that I didn't need the procedure. She consented to doctors slicing my heart open.

"Do whatever you got to do," Debra used to say to all experiments that the doctors wanted to try on me. She always gave them the green light to do what their heart desired instead of what I wanted.

I was sure she must have also told the doctors the same thing that time. It was horrible to know that the person responsible for me during that time took my life for granted.

The doctors also confirmed my suspicion by telling me that Debra had told them to proceed with the surgery. She didn't hesitate a second while permitting them to slice open my heart.

I knew it would be over once they went for my heart. I might have come back from the coma, but I couldn't make it if they had put me on an operation table to perform such invasive surgery on me.

I made it very clear that I didn't want them to operate on me. I wasn't going to let them experiment on my body and try methods that could potentially ruin my health or take my life. But I was helpless and alone.

It was only me there and no one else.

I was at the disposal of those doctors, and they played with me like a puppet. I had lost all autonomy and authority in my life, and now those people in white coats were steering my life in whatever direction they wanted.

When I recall that horrible episode, I remember that it was only Debra and me. There was no one else around who was in my family, and Debra was hardly acting like family.

While in a coma, I had no idea who had visited me. I was someplace else, and it was terrifying. But then I woke up one day, and I was unable to move my body. On top of everything, the doctors were preparing to do an operation on me. So I needed someone to be on my side during that horrifying time.

I didn't know if anyone was going to come to my rescue. I couldn't move or escape the hospital. I needed solid support from a family member, something Debra would never do. I finally had a faint hope when my son, Rob, decided to fly to Fresno to save me.

Rob was living in San Diego while I was admitted to the hospital. Rob was 22 at that time, and my daughter was 20. They were old enough to protect their father. The doctors and Debra assumed that I was on my own and that they could do anything they wanted with me since I didn't have anyone to look out for me there.

That's where they were wrong. I wasn't alone. I had my own family, and they wouldn't give up on me so easily.

When my son, Rob, found out that I was going to have a heart operation against my wishes, he arrived there to stop it from happening. So finally, I had the support I needed.

It took an eight-hour train from San Diego to reach Fresno. Rob and my brother-in-law- Damon Robertson Sr., decided to check up on me in Fresno. They hopped on the train and finally took the long journey to reach the hospital.

My son wanted to make sure that his father was okay and that he was getting the treatment he needed. The only source of information for my son was my sister, Debra, and she was the last person who could be trusted.

The doctors thought that she was the one who was responsible for me since she was family, except that she was anything but family. She wasn't there to serve my interest. She had far different intentions than what was expected of her.

I often think about what would have happened if they hadn't taken the train ride. Perhaps, I wouldn't even be here to tell my story and how God helped me in that dark place if they hadn't come down there to save me.

Rob and Damon came to the hospital where I was staying and met the doctors. They discussed my condition with them and tried to tell him how they needed to operate on my heart. Rob knew I didn't want this operation, so he was determined to stop the doctors.

The doctors told them that the procedure they were about to carry out was exploratory. Something about that word was extremely triggering. There I was, stuck to a hospital bed, paralyzed from the neck down, unable to make any basic movement, and there were the doctors who wanted to do nothing but carry out experiments on me.

It was disturbing that out of everything in my body that needed treatment; they chose my heart to operate on. It was very risky for someone who had just been in a coma and was paralyzed. The risks didn't matter to them. They were talking about the heart surgery like it was something minor and wouldn't affect me that much.

Their words still linger in my mind. All those procedures and surgeries were exploratory, and they had no intention to diagnose and then treat me properly, which was exactly what I needed instead of their experiments.

Finally, the doctors relented and called off the operation. Now, it was clear that they didn't have my or my family's consent. It took my son, flying from another city all the way to Fresno, to get to the hospital to listen to me.

I have no idea what they would have done to me if my son hadn't shown up. Perhaps, they would have dissected my heart, and I wouldn't be here today. But Rob came in at the right time to stop the surgery from happening, and it worked in my favor.

God himself intended the arrival of my son and brother-in-law. I wouldn't have been here if they didn't arrive in time to stop the operation. That's how I knew that God was still with me, and he was sending the help I needed desperately.

God gave me my children, and my son was there to rescue his father. I was blessed with my children's love; their love proved stronger than the conspiracy against me.

The doctors might not have gotten the chance to operate on my heart, but they still weren't backing down. They put me through painful procedures, which added to my agony.

They did a procedure on me which required a camera to go down my throat. I was made to swallow the camera that went inside my body. I was terrified of the procedure. Nevertheless, I was forced to go through it. It was extremely painful, but nobody cared if I was in pain.

They kept treating me like a frog in a laboratory.

I had a brother named Mark. I called him while I was in Fresno and I told him what was happening. The hospital was terrible, and they were constantly treating me like I was an experiment for them. I wanted him to come down there and save me from all the torture.

I cried on the call. I was hysterical. I needed my family to be there for me. The doctors had to know that I wasn't alone and had support, but it wasn't the case. I told him that he needed to come there to save me or they would keep playing with my life, but to my surprise, it didn't affect him.

*"These people are trying to kill me; please come here. I need you,"* I begged him.

It didn't make any difference. After hearing me cry and beg him to come to save me, he just left me there. There was no hint of consolation.

My brother didn't show up when I needed him the most.

Following the conversation with my brother, I called up my nephews as well. Well, they didn't show up either. It felt like all of them had given up on me.

He never came to see me. It was like my misery didn't matter to him. We shared the bond of blood, but it did not mean anything to him.

As I was stuck in the hospital bed, I realized why the ghetto hospital was so notorious. It was infamous for all the right reasons. Your first job as a doctor is to reassure the patient about his health and give him hope. But unfortunately, the doctors at the ghetto hospital were contrary to how one expects a doctor to be. They were unkind to me, and it seemed like they were purposely mean to their patients.

After spending four weeks in the hospital in Fresno, I was moved to a hospital in San Diego. The ghetto hospital in Fresno was a horrible experience, and I was now hoping for relief.

I was terrified about what was going to happen to me. I was a healthy person, and now I was stuck in the hospital. I couldn't move my hands or feet. I was chained to the hospital bed constantly.

I was an outdoorsy person who didn't like to remain indoors for a long time, but alas! Life had something else planned out for me.

Walking, running, or meeting my friends over the weekend had become a dream for me.

Could I ever walk again?

Did I have any hope left?

The doctors didn't believe I was going to make it. They were pretty sure that there was no hope for me. Whenever I asked them about my condition, they told me that I was going to die.

No one wants to hear that they will die, even if they are dying. People need hope to survive, but the doctors tried to steal whatever remaining hope I had. When I felt that excruciating pain in my back, I didn't know I would end up there.

I believed that a good hospital could find a way to cure my pain, and I could walk again. But then my sister shook me to the core of my existence when she took me to the ghetto hospital and left me there to die.

What those doctors used to say to me still echoes in my mind.

"You're going to die," they'd tell me. They said it with so much conviction that I almost believed them. I was expecting death at any moment. I was certain that they weren't there to cure me; they had already given up on me.

When I think about death, I go back to the time I was in a coma and had all those nightmares. I didn't know if it was real, but it was absolutely horrible. I thought I was not going to make it. It was one nightmare after the other. There was no escape, and I was stuck. I thought I was trapped and couldn't be helped anymore.

That experience is what death felt like to me. But then I came back to life. I was finally out of the coma and realized it was just a series of nightmares. It might have been terrifying, but I had somehow made it back to real life.

If I could do it once, I could do it again.

The doctors might have been trying to convince me that my life was ending and there was no cure for me, but I didn't stop believing. I was not someone who accepted defeat.

I was a fighter.

I never bowed down to challenges, and I wasn't going to do that this time again.

It was heartbreaking to hear those words coming out of the doctors' mouths. They were the last people I expected to hear it from. I deserved support and treatment as any other person did. I didn't deserve their cruelty. They thought I would die, so they could say anything they wanted.

I had my phases of hopelessness when I believed what the doctors said. I thought about the possibility of not making it. I was not that old yet and had so much to do in my life and for my kids. I kept telling myself that I had to survive for my children.

I couldn't just leave them on their own. I had to do everything to fight my situation. I couldn't leave my family behind as Debra had left me. I had no other option than to fight.

Debra's behavior had started getting even more suspicious after I had woken up from the coma. But, perhaps, she didn't see it coming. She must have thought I was gone for good, but I wasn't.

I was still there.

I might not have been able to move my body anymore, but I had fought the coma and could also fight this. All I had to was keep believing, so I did that.

There is no doubt that I was in a dark pit, and there was hardly any hope left to climb out of it. I had been ditched in that pit by someone very close to me. This was someone I had trusted with all my heart, but they had been planning my downfall all along. Unfortunately, I had been blind to this person's intentions as I didn't allow myself to see what was in front of me.

It was none other than my dear sister, Debra herself.

I started having doubts about her intentions when she was talking to the paramedics' guy, but my suspicions only grew stronger after each passing minute. She had cleverly planned to take me to the ghetto hospital against my will. Of course, I had no say in that situation, and she got what she wanted.

I went back over that night in Debra's house when my whole world was turned upside down. I was perfectly fine before coming over to her place. I didn't feel sick at all. So I can certainly say that I was healthy before visiting her. However, it was after meeting her that everything went downhill. Something had happened between the time she had gone to get the drinks and returned.

It was at that very moment that the pain started, and I collapsed.

One thing was for sure: I was staying in that hospital for a while. It wasn't something that would take a few weeks to cure. I was paralyzed, and I couldn't move my body. It was something severe. I started confronting the fact that this hospital would be my home for a long time.

I wished that my parents were there to support me like they always did. They were the kindest people I knew. I never felt alone or threatened until they were alive. Their memories were still alive in my mind.

I needed them so badly. If I could do anything to bring them back, I would. They were people of extremely strong characters. They weren't built like the usual people. They had their core belief and stuck to them.

Losing my parents was the most heartbreaking experience of my life. I could have never imagined losing them, but I did. I thought about how painful it was and compared it to my paralysis. The loss of my parents hurt me more than the paralysis did.

They fought with every difficult situation so easily that you couldn't even tell they were worried. They were gone, but they had left their spirit behind. I could feel that their spirit was providing the strength to keep up. I had the best parents in the world, so I tried to remember them during my time of challenges. They were my best friends and mentors. I don't know what would have happened to me if it wasn't for my parents' strength.

I would think about what my parents would do in this situation.

I knew that my parents would have bowed down to other people. They would have fought hard against all odds until they had made it. That's what I had to do.

I had to keep fighting.

# Chapter 5:
# Poway Healthcare Center

I spent four weeks in the hospital in Fresno, where they treated me like a lab rat. I don't know how I got through that horrible time, but somehow, I did. Every day was the same. I never heard them telling me that I might get better.

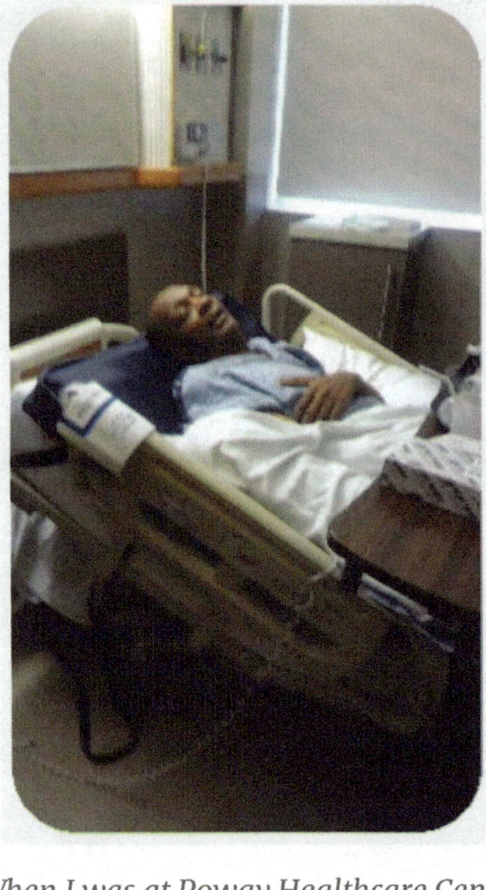

*When I was at Poway Healthcare Center*

*"You're very sick."*

*"You're going to die."*

I kept hearing those words almost every day. After getting diced constantly for four weeks in that ghetto hospital, I was finally moved to another place.

I don't remember the day I was moved. I absolutely don't have any recollection of the day. I was going through a testing time, and my reality was blurry. It was not easy for me to keep track of time when I was staying there.

The only thing I remember is that I woke up in an unfamiliar place. I woke up and saw that my surroundings had changed. I thought I was in another ward, but that wasn't it.

It was a very dark room. I could hardly make out anything because of the vision shadowed by the darkness. I saw two people in the room I was staying in. They differed from the doctors and nurses assigned to me back in Fresno.

The doctors might have knocked me out because I didn't remember moving to a new place. When I woke up, I went into a panic attack. I was out of control and couldn't think straight. I was screaming and crying.

It was Poway Healthcare Center. It wasn't a hospital where I was sent to receive better treatment. It was a nursing home, and I had been sent there to die.

The doctors didn't have any hope for me and never let me believe I could get better. All dreams and aspirations had been stolen from me. I might have been moved to San Diego, but that didn't mean I was about to get the treatment I deserved.

They were waiting for me to die.

I was a hopeless case for the doctors, and cases like mine are often referred to nursing homes. These facilities have people to take care of people who stay there. Most of them were old and sick people. I was one of the sick ones without any hope of recovery.

I was told I had been moved there so I could spend the time I had left peacefully. I knew that I had been given a death sentence and was simply moved there so I could die.

I still couldn't move any part of my body. I couldn't stand, hold, sit, or pee. I was completely paralyzed from the neck down. There was no movement. The only activity I was left with was lying on the bed and watching the ceiling.

I couldn't do basic tasks such as eating with my own hands or going to the washroom. I had a catheter attached so I could pee through it. An adult's diaper was wrapped around me so I could pass stool. It was a disgusting feeling.

While my body was paralyzed, my brain was working perfectly fine. I still had my senses intact and could think properly.

I remember the doctors going through the notes from the hospital in Fresno. I heard some mumbles from them talking to each other about how they had declared I was going to die.

*"Mr. Halliburton, you're never going to walk again,"* they told me.

I was dependent on other people to clean me and feed me. I was a really tall man. I was 6'5 and it was beyond me that someone who used to behave with so much strength was now depending on others for the tiniest task.

I couldn't see any development while I was in the nursing home. I was getting weaker every day. My health was getting worse, and nobody expected any improvement in the coming times.

I used to stare at the ceiling and walls all the time. I would think about the life I had only a month ago. It was fulfilling. I could walk, sit, eat and be present with my loved ones. I missed my children and friends. I was completely alone in that place, confined to four walls.

The experience was extremely damaging to my mental health because I was not a person who liked to be confined to a bed. I had never been into staying in bed all day and not getting up to do anything. I was an energetic man who never felt lazy to do anything.

I was a paraplegic. I was ready to take on all sorts of physical challenges. The life I had haunted while I was confined to the bed in the nursing home. I thought about how I took that life for granted.

The realization hit me like a truck.

We take our blessings from God for granted every day because we never imagine what will happen to us if we are deprived of our physical abilities. We wait around and sulk because we feel lazy. We think we have all the time in the world, but we don't. Life can take a different turn at any given point.

That's the thing about life.

It doesn't remain the same.

I used to talk about how I was going to walk again. I was certain about changing my fate. The word traveled to the doctors, who weren't happy about it. One day the doctor visited me and appeared to be serious.

*"You should stop telling people you're going to walk again. It's going to demotivate you. You're only hurting yourself,"* I remember the doctor's words clearly even today.

*"I am going to walk again,"* I looked the doctor in the eye as I uttered those words with complete faith in God.

*"No, you're not. You're only going to end up messing with your mental health like this,"* she responded.

Little did these doctors know what God had planned for me.

I used to think about my parents all the time. I used to ask myself what they would do in my situation. They would have fought with everything they had. Yes, that's who my parents were. I learned how to believe and fight from my parents. They might have been gone, but I wasn't going to let them down.

I had to keep fighting.

The worst part of my situation was that I was alone. I had been left to die, and nobody cared to check up on me. I believe I had been a good father and friend, but when it came to looking out for me, I had no one.

I was falling down into a dark pit, and there was no one I was familiar with around me. The least my family and friends could do for me was offer their support, but apparently, that was too much to ask for. Nobody cared to visit me on my supposed death bed.

I had invested a great deal of time in building relationships with people. I cared for them. I would have definitely shown up if my loved one had been in my place. Instead, I never received any empathy from the people around me.

I thought my life was over when my family members started giving up on me. They didn't believe that I was going to make it. They could have simply tried to believe, but they chose otherwise.

I was on my own, and the awareness of the cruel reality had hit me hard. Debra was with me from the beginning of my torment, and she played an important role in what was about to happen to me.

Her role in the situation in Fresno had already become suspicious, but I was still holding on to the hope of her at least trying to give me courage or support during my ordeal.

When you're going through trials and tribulations, it's only natural to expect people close to you to stick around. They have been there with you during the good times, so it's only fair that you receive their support when you're going through something horrible.

I learned this the hard way that the people who had benefitted me when I was healthy decided to abandon me when I could provide them with nothing. I wasn't asking them for anything more than their support and courage, yet they turned their back on me as if I'd asked them for their belongings.

My movement was limited owing to the paralysis, so I couldn't just walk up to people and ask why they couldn't spare time for me when I needed them the most. I was lying in bed waiting for my death and couldn't find any sign of support.

Out of every time I was abandoned by my loved ones, the one that shocked me the most was when I talked to Rosalynd. She was my best friend for 25 years. We had a very platonic friendship, but I loved her more than anyone. She was my rock and biggest support.

I met her when she was a 19-year-old girl in LA, and I was 22. We were very young and naive. Soon we became friends and then best friends. Rosalynd and I developed a bond that remained strong throughout our life.

We both went about our lives, fell in love with other people, and got married and divorced as well, but our friendship stuck throughout. I got married and divorced twice during our friendship, yet her friendship with me remained a package. I was fine until I had her.

She was my rock.

I had my fair share of ups and downs and heartbreaks, but Rosalynd somehow always remained a part of my life. I knew I was going to be fine as long as I had her. We would laugh, cry and share everything about our lives.

Rosalynd got divorced. She later moved to Florida. Distance had never been an obstacle in our relationship. We would often call each other and keep talking for long hours. We would talk about our lives, feelings, and every little event that happened throughout the day. She was someone I could never get tired of talking to.

Sometimes we would talk through the night, and she would fall asleep, yet I remained awake. I could hear her falling asleep quietly and breathing over the phone. It was as if she was right there with me, and the distance would vanish.

She was the center of my world. I loved her more than I ever loved both of my wives. That love meant something. We had been platonic friends for more than two decades. We were both separated from our partners, and with everything we shared, I really thought that we were in love.

I wanted to move to Florida for her so we could be together. I could have done anything for her. You name it. I could have even taken a bullet for her because that was how much I loved her.

She was my everything.

When I was lying there paralyzed, I used to think about her. I would imagine how all my pain would go away if I could see her just once. I needed her to be around me. Perhaps I would've felt less hurt. Her support was the only thing I wanted. I didn't ask for much.

Then came the day I called her up. I told her everything. I told her how I was paralyzed and couldn't move. I let her know that I didn't have anyone with me.

I thought the first thing she would do was to come and see me. But that's not what happened.

She disappeared.

She was my best friend, and I needed her badly, but instead of being there for me, she gave up on me. I never heard from her. It was heartbreaking. The abandonment left me feeling like I didn't mean anything to her. More than two decades of friendship meant nothing to her when her friend actually needed her.

She lived in Florida. I didn't expect her to fly to me, but the least I expected was for her to check up on me, but she couldn't even do the bare minimum for the friend who would have done it every day for her.

All I wanted was to hear her voice. That's all. That's all I asked for. I just wanted to know that she was there. I thought if I could hear her again, I would be fine.

When she gave up on me, it felt like I had died. Coma and nightmares weren't anything compared to the pain she gave me. Being abandoned by someone I thought was my world was equivalent to death.

We used to tell each other that no matter what happened, we would never leave each other. And I intended to keep that promise. I never doubted for a second that she would leave me.

*"Don't ever leave my life,"* she used to tell me, and that was a promise I held on to. I was never going to break that promise. I would have died for her, and I mean it.

She broke the promise she made to the person who never gave up on her. Her abandonment felt more like a divorce than anything because we had been friends for most of our lives. I spent a great deal of time with her. All gone in a second.

Years later, we spoke on the phone. To my surprise, she talked to me as if nothing had happened. It didn't even matter to her. She never realized that she had broken my heart.

I asked her the dreadful question that had broken me apart when she left me to fend for myself.

*"Why did you just leave me alone?"* I finally asked her, hoping for some closure after all the hurt she had caused me.

"I thought you were going to be fine," that was the explanation she had for leaving me behind and never checking up on me.

She was the person that broke my heart in peace because she promised she would never leave, but she did. I cannot even begin to count the times I cried because of her.

She killed a part of me when she abandoned me.

I believe that every kind of pain can be eased down if your loved ones support you. You need to know that the people you rely on care for you. I also wished that I received the care I deserved, but unfortunately, it didn't happen in my case.

People who were close to me let me down big time. They bailed on me when I needed them the most. It wasn't something I was expecting from my family and friends. I didn't want to be in that place alone. The solitude made my heart break every day.

I would see other people's families coming to visit them. They would look after their family member and laugh with them. I didn't have anyone to do that for me. I was alone and didn't have anyone I could count on.

My friend of 10 years came to visit me one day, but it didn't end well. He was constantly making fun of me and my situation. I was paralyzed. I couldn't sit or walk; it was all just a big joke to him.

*"You really can't walk,"* he mocked me as he saw me in a wheelchair.

I was shocked. He was supposed to make me feel better, but he made me feel even worse. I cried after he left.

How can you mock someone who has lost their ability to function physically?

It was cruel of him. He had been friends with me for a decade, and my condition was a joke to him. He didn't care what effect his words would have on me. I cried a lot after he left.

One of the people who constantly called to check on me was my other sister Monica. She was a few years younger than me and had always been a very kind and giving woman. She was my support when I felt like I had no one. I was extremely close to her, so her presence did wonders for my mental health.

Monica used to live in Milwaukee, Wisconsin. It was far for her, but she still managed to call the nurses and doctors almost daily. Monica remained my No.1 person when it came to supporting me. Whenever I felt like giving up, she was always there to tell me to hang in there and keep believing in God.

She often reminded me to keep praying to God to make me walk again. She believed that God had the power to turn the worst situation into a miracle. It was her belief that instilled faith in me. Every time I was in pain, I thought about God. I felt his presence all around me.

I would wake up in a frenzy when I would realize that I couldn't move my legs. It was heartbreaking to wake up every day to find my still body unable to function like it was supposed to.

I would often throw fits when the realization of my paralysis dawned on me. Monica would hold my hand and try to make me understand that I could not lose hope.

"Trust God, please trust God," her words still echo in my mind.

Those words, Monica had so much power. It was not just something she was saying to console me. Those words meant a great deal as they made me believe that I had to trust God as He was the only one who could help me.

Monica was the only person who never gave up on me while I was stuck in that bed. She had faith in God and me. She became my lifeline while I was fighting to make it.

I was missing some of the belongings that I needed at the hospital. Debra was the only family member living in Fresno, so I decided to call her and ask her to bring my belongings to the hospital, but little did I know what would follow after I had called her.

I couldn't move, so I asked the nurse to make a call for me. The nurse brought the phone and put it on speaker. The nurse put the phone on my chest so I could talk to my sister. It was all too difficult to contemplate. I couldn't even do basic tasks such as making calls. I was completely dependent on other people to help me out.

The nurse was helpful and helped me through the entire calling process. The call rang for a while, and then finally, Debra picked it up.

I had decided to get some of the important stuff that belonged to me. I needed some documents related to business and other things as well. I worked very hard for twenty years, and all the documents related to my work were lying somewhere covered in dust. I needed them with me.

I never asked for much as I didn't like to bother people around me. I thought that Debra would at least help me out. It wasn't such a big deal. I wasn't asking for money. It was simply my belongings. I never intended to ask her to bring my belongings to the hospital. I thought she could help give my belongings to someone who could bring them to San Diego since she lived in Fresno.

I had my clothes back at Fresno, documents, and a custom-made fur coat. But the most important belonging that I needed was my mother's Bible. I needed it more than anything else when I was in Poway Healthcare. The Bible was very close to my mother, one of the few belongings she left behind when she passed away.

It was not precious jewels or money that I yearned for. It was the Bible I wished for when my mother departed.

Debra's tone was cold and repulsive.

She started getting angry, and I didn't know what to do. She was furious at me and kept yelling. The phone was on speaker, so it wasn't just me listening to her.

She didn't sound like my sister.

She started calling me names and derogatory ones. It was horrible to hear her cursing at me as I was lying in that hospital bed, paralyzed. She didn't care that I might not make it. She kept going and continued cursing me.

She pierced my heart with her cruel words. I couldn't take it anymore and broke down. I was sobbing, hearing my sister curse me. I couldn't do anything except cry.

I couldn't yell.

I couldn't move.

I begged Debra not to treat me like I was an enemy. But she didn't listen to me for a second. I kept crying on the call. She could hear all that, but it made her any kinder.

She was still brutal.

I told Debra to spare me the unkindness. I told her that I had been in a coma. I was fighting for my life. It was not the time to break my spirit.

"Please don't do this, Debra," I pleaded with my sister as she continued cursing.

What followed was even more horrible. It was just the beginning of how cruel she could get.

She sent me a picture of myself in a coma. I was lying in a bed like a lifeless body. I didn't understand why she would do such a horrible thing to me.

It was inhumane.

"Look at you, you're shit," she captioned the picture.

I couldn't believe that my sister was mocking my struggle to live. It felt like my life was a joke to her. She didn't try to understand how it would break my heart.

When I saw the picture, I lost my composure. I was taken aback by the visuals. It almost felt like she wanted me to be in that state. She enjoyed my misery was shoving my suffering in my face.

The phone fell off my chest when I saw the picture.

I couldn't bear the misery. Like the pain wasn't enough already, Debra put me in such a horrible situation. I didn't understand how someone could do such a cruel thing to her own brother.

I knew she had done something to me. It wasn't just her anger. It was her revealing who she truly was.

I had no idea what was happening, but she finally started showing her colors. All I wanted were my belongings, but she was extremely hostile to me. That phone call was crucial for me to realize what had been happening all along. I already had my suspicions, but Debra's reaction made me start believing that it was not just a doubt.

She was making it pretty clear that she was not on my side.

It wasn't my sister who was talking. It was someone else. Someone who had been lurking in the corner, looking for the right moment to come for me.

It was at that moment that I realized that Debra was the one who had poisoned me. It was not just in my head anymore. All the clues were pointing in her direction. She had been leaving crumbs in her trail as she tried to kill her own brother.

I could have never imagined that my own sister would do something so vile to take my life from me. It took me time to come to terms with what I'd witnessed, but I slowly started picking up the clues she had been dropping all along.

My own sister had poisoned me.

I had been left with nothing. I looked around for hope and realized that God was around me. I might not have my loved one's support, but I had God. He provided me with the strength I needed to fight the situation. I knew that he was there because how else was I still alive?

I was still breathing. I could talk, see, and cry. I could express my emotions. I cried to God. I asked him for mercy. I knew God wouldn't leave me alone like the rest of the people. My loved ones left me alone to die in the nursing home.

But God hadn't left me alone. He wanted me to fight everything. He wanted me to stay alive. I had to make it for him. I felt his presence in my bones. I might have lost everything, but I had God. As long as I had him, I didn't need anyone else.

I would talk to God like he was a friend. I didn't have anyone else to talk to, but he was always there. I believe that he had been listening to me all along. He knew the agony I was being put through. He was aware that I didn't have anyone. That's why he gave me strength by faith so I could find a reason to stay alive.

My bond with God grew stronger during my paralysis. I realized that, after all, I wasn't dependent on anyone. God had decided my fate, and no power in the world could defeat me if he wanted me to make it.

I asked God to put an end to my suffering.

I asked Him for mercy every day.

I saw that people other than me in the nursing home were mostly older than me or in a wheelchair. The nursing home had some good people as well on their staff who helped me throughout my journey.

I had a physiotherapist named Neil, who used to encourage me throughout. He was a tough man and had a style of a military man. He told me that I could do anything if I had the mental state to provide the strength.

Neil was tough on me. He never pitied me; instead, he wanted me to get better. He believed that I could recover if I kept working toward improving my mobility.

Every day, my job was to get better. Whether it was trying to move a limb or finger, Neil wanted me to keep trying. It was not easy to attempt something which I supposed I wasn't physically able to do, but Neil motivated me to keep trying.

A guy who used to be an assistant of a nurse would play music, and it caught my attention. The music he played was soothing and filled me with hope. The rhythm made me want to keep going. So every time he would play music, I would feel motivated.

While I was staying in the nursing home, a nurse started noticing me. She noticed how I was always alone and had no visitors. So she started coming to check up on how I was doing. She wanted to make sure that I was doing well. It warmed my heart to see that someone still cared for me.

I was so lonely that the bare minimum care used to warm up my heart. I wanted to have someone by my side who cared about me. She was someone who actually started caring about me when she saw me suffering.

I would wait for her to come so I could talk to her. She would talk to me about her life and mine. She spent a great deal of time with me, which was exactly what I needed at that point.

She knew that I didn't have any family support, so she started treating me like her family. She would change my diaper, massage my head, cut my hair, and clean me up. She would make sure that I was cleaned up and never left me unattended.

We would often discuss what was going on outside the four walls of that room. She was my only source of connection to the outside world. She would tell me interesting news, and I would feel like I was still a part of the world.

I can still remember the moment I was crying because I was alone in that place, and none of my loved ones would come to visit me. But one person was there, and it was one of the nurses. She saw me breaking down, and sadness clenched my existence. That's when she said the words that restored my faith in life.

"I'll be your family," her words echoed in my mind since I was completely alone.

I didn't believe there was going to come to a point in my life when I could walk again, but she reassured me that I would walk again. She had faith in me and life. It was a blessing at that moment to hear something so kind in the midst of my solitude.

I believe that some people care for others because they have been blessed with empathy. They don't seek any benefits. I was definitely not in a position to help anyone with anything. In fact, I was the one who needed help. The nurse stuck by my side during the next one and a half years I spent in that place.

She had made me her family.

I finally had someone who was looking out for me.

# Chapter 6: Holy Intervention

I believe my spiritual connection with God started developing while I was in a coma. I might have been unresponsive, but something inside me was still alive and fighting. My spirit transcended the realm of nightmares and dreams while I was in a coma.

My body was no longer controlling my life; then, what was it that kept me alive throughout?

It was my spirit that had taken over. I was going to all these places in my head. I was caught up in a battle, and my spirit was trying to help me navigate the turbulent waters.

When I woke up and was moved to Poway Healthcare Center, I felt God's presence everywhere.

He was there when I was in a coma.

He was there when I woke up to find that my body was paralyzed.

He was there when my best friend abandoned me.

He was there when Debra humiliated me.

I might have felt alone, but I was never left alone by God. He was present with me at every step during my condition. I was hurt, not only physically, but emotionally as well. My heart was broken by people I hoped would never leave my side. I thought I would be left alone when people gave up on me, but God had other plans for me. He never stopped looking out for me.

My tears wouldn't stop flowing down. It was all the hurt and heartbreak that was strangling me all along. It was building up every day while I was in that place. I wanted to become whole again. I had never done anyone wrong.

As the days went by, I didn't stop speaking to God. He became a friend who I could always count on. I would talk to him about my pain and how much it hurt me to be stuck in one place, incapable of moving my body.

My heart was filled with grief. I would scream in agony all the time. I didn't know what else to do. I felt as if I was the loneliest person in the world. I used to miss being able to run and feel the breeze on my neck. I missed having my favorite food with my own hands. I missed hugging the people I loved. I missed having the freedom to go anywhere in the world.

I often thought about why I was stripped of a healthy life. I had been doing so well before that incident in Fresno. I wished I could go back and live my life like I used to. There were so many instances when I took life's blessings for granted, and I yearned to have a chance at living my life freely once again.

I kept trying to fight because I believed He didn't want me to give up. He would have never made me stay alive if he wanted me to accept defeat. He was responsible for every breath I took, and I knew he wouldn't abandon me.

I would close my eyes and imagine everything I would do if God gave me the strength to walk again. God has sent all those people to help me in my struggle. Whether it was the nurse, Neil, or my sister, Monica, they wanted me to keep trying regardless of what anyone else had to say.

As I kept speaking to God and keeping my faith strong, I became certain that it was not the end of the road. God had the power to turn every situation around if He intended.

I would remember what Monica used to tell me about keeping my faith strong. She believed in me, and I knew that I also had to keep believing if I wanted to be able to walk once again.

People don't realize what they have got until they have lost it. We take every blessing for granted since it's something that seems regular to us, and we don't try to comprehend what if those blessings were to be taken away from us. We chase after what we don't have and forget what we have, which makes us ungrateful.

I realized how important those blessings were in my life now that they had been seized. I wanted to get out of that place and breathe fresh air. I spoke to God about how I yearned for him to bless me with a miracle. It was only Him that could save me now.

There were nights when I would weep all night thinking about my situation. I used to get overwhelmed with all the loss I had to endure ever since I went to Fresno to visit Debra. My situation was a constant reminder of the opportunities, blessings, and love I had lost.

For a year and a half, all I did was cry and yell in agony. I was miserable and couldn't get better, no matter how hard I tried. I didn't lose hope, yet it hurt me to wake up and realize where I was. There were moments when I felt I would stay in that place for the rest of my life.

I told God that if He blessed me with a miracle, I promised to show everybody what he did for me. I was determined to show the world how God had blessed me and what he could do for others. I was firm in my promise to God. I meant everything I spoke to him about.

Then came the day when my life was about to encounter something that nobody would have seen coming. It was Sunday, and I was lying in bed, speaking to God.

Suddenly, I heard two voices speaking. The voice was very faint and seemed like two people were having a conversation, but there was no one in the room. I listened carefully only to realize that it was not two people but spirits. I held my heart, trying to figure out what was happening.

When I first heard the voices, it scared the shit out of me. I didn't know what was happening or where these voices came from. I thought I was having another mental breakdown.

*Am I dreaming?*

*I must be dreaming.*

*It can't be real.*

I realized that the two spirits were none other than God and Jesus Himself. They were speaking to each other, and they were talking about me. My heart started beating fast, and I couldn't contain the excitement. God had been listening to me all along.

I heard that they were talking about giving me another chance in life. They wanted me to have my life back again. I couldn't believe what I was witnessing.

*"Do you believe I can heal you?"* I was asked by God.

*"Yes, yes, yes!"* I yelled.

I felt the spirit enter my body and surround me with its holy presence. I could feel it in my soul. The spirit was there, and it was talking to me. God asked me if I believed that He could help me. I told him that I believed in him and all he was capable of doing.

For a moment, I also felt that God touched me. It was an astounding experience, and I didn't know how to react.

I felt something in my hands that I hadn't felt before. It had been a long time since I felt that. It was movement. After a long time of struggle and praying, I could finally feel something for the first time.

It was hard to believe that I was witnessing movement again since the doctors in Fresno had told me that I would die. There was no hope for me, yet here I was, witnessing the presence of the spirit of Jesus, who had blessed me with hope at life once again.

I constantly went back and forth between coma and consciousness, so I didn't know it was real. I had wanted my body to feel something so bad that I feared that I was simply dreaming about it, and I would wake up to find that it was not reality.

It was when the nurse saw my hand. She was surprised to see that my fingers were moving. She looked at me, all shocked since she couldn't believe her eyes. I had been brought there to die, so no one expected that I would be able to move again.

It was too good to be true. I could feel something in my hand, but I needed someone to tell me that it was actually happening. I was longing for reassurance.

*"You're moving your fingers,"* the nurse finally said, and those words changed my life.

It was real.

I was actually moving my finger. A miracle had happened against all odds. I wasn't dreaming anymore. It was the reality. God had given me another chance at life. After all, my prayers were not in vain.

Although I always hoped that I would be able to move once again, it was a surprise to me as well. We all hope for the best and keep believing, but what I did differently was keep my faith in God. I knew that if I held on to Him, He would bless me one day.

That moment reaffirmed my belief in God and that He was on my side. A lot of people had given up on me. They had abandoned me since they believed the end was approaching, and there was no hope for me.

I had spent endless nights crying to God. I would cry every time my loved ones gave up on me. I felt alone, abandoned, and betrayed. I had invested so many years into building those relationships, yet it didn't take a moment for them to turn their back on me when I needed them the most.

When people I believed would be there for me left me behind, the people in the nursing home reaffirmed me. They were the ones who made it their goal to motivate me to get better, while the people close to me mocked me for my condition.

God was watching everything. He saw how my heart was broken by the ones whom I loved, the ones, and He also saw how people who didn't share any relationship with me made me believe that I could make it if I had just kept trying.

Only a while ago, I was lying in a hospital bed in Fresno where they kept experimenting on my body, and yet here I was, finally gaining control of my body.

I would always remember the people and doctors who visited me in Fresno hospital and how they would mock my situation and tell me I was going to die. I knew that it was not the end. I couldn't go away so easily. I believed in the miracle of God, and I was certain that He would have mercy on me.

All those nights of crying and screaming had finally started to come to an end. The long night of misery was over. The movement I felt in my hand wasn't just a feeling. It was a miracle that symbolized what God could do when you keep faith in Him.

That slight movement in my hand gave me back the hope I had been losing. It was only because God was so merciful to me that I went from a hopeless condition to regaining control of my movement.

If I had believed in those people who kept telling me that my situation was hopeless and I was going to die, then I would never make it that far. It might have been a small movement for the spectators, but that small movement embodied all the hope I needed to live.

All I needed was a sign from God that He was there — watching me. I had finally received the sign from God. He answered my prayers and gave me another chance to take control of my destiny.

I thought about that moment when I was forcefully taken to the ghetto hospital in Fresno. I felt like I had lost control of my life and my destiny had been stolen from me. God was the one who made me believe that no one could ever steal my life from me, as He was the one who had the authority to decide my destiny.

At that moment, I knew that God hadn't left me alone, and He wanted me to keep fighting, and that's what I was going to do.

# Chapter 7: A Failed Medical System

I hadn't seen any improvement until I witnessed God reaching out to me to give me another chance at life. Something clicked in me out of nowhere when I first managed to move my finger.

Before my interaction with God happened, I used to cry myself to sleep. I had a catheter to help me pee. I was wrapped in a diaper so that I could pass stool. I needed someone else to change my diaper; otherwise, I would lie in my own waste for hours.

It wasn't just my condition that gave me nightmares. It was also my surroundings. I was staying with people who were very old and extremely sick. Some of them were living out the last days of their lives in that nursing home. It was heartbreaking to see them getting weaker and sicker every day.

These people were nearing death, and everyone else around them had to just watch them go. I was not spared the cruel torture of watching people I had known pass away as we were all staying together in the nursing home.

Sometimes, I would start to get to know someone and discover a little more about their lives before they were moved to the nursing home, and then, I would find out that they had passed away.

I was witnessing so many deaths that it started traumatizing me. I was watching a fate that might happen to me any day. During those times, Monica constantly reminded me to keep my faith strong in God. If it weren't for her, I wouldn't have been able to stay strong in the face of everything.

The improvement I had started noticing was owed to God, who showed me mercy. Moving my fingers was the first step of my journey. It might not have appeared as a significant development in my case, but it was a huge achievement for me. I had been told by so many people that I would never be able to move my body.

There was a person during the challenging times who became my spiritual support. It was none other than Carolyn Anderson. She had been my friend for the last fifteen years.

Carolyn was a person of faith. She had very firm beliefs about Christianity and had practiced it with all her heart. When Carolyn found out about my trials, she did her best to help me through the course of spiritual healing. She put me in a prayer group where my bond with God developed to become stronger.

She started making strong prayers for my health. She would make sure she wouldn't miss any opportunity to pray for my life, which worked miracles for me.

All those prayers and conversations with God hadn't been in vain. He was listening to me all along, and it was clear that He wanted me to get better. I couldn't give up now. My faith in God strengthened after that incident, and it became the biggest support I needed to continue my progress.

I wasn't alone in my journey. The nurse, trainer, and physical therapist worked on my recovery. I was motivated by the support I was receiving in that place. It was the first time I felt I wasn't alone because I knew God was with me. He was sending me the motivation I needed.

It's amazing how everything in your surroundings starts working in your favor when you once set your mind on something. I had been constantly sliced and diced back in Fresno, yet all it took was a sign from God and His mercy to make the impossible happen.

One of the many aspects that started working in my favor was music. Yes, it was something as simple as that. There was a member of the staff who would play music while working. Now that I had started moving my hand, my mind also started catching up with music.

I used to be a very good dancer back in the day. I loved dancing and would groove for hours. It was part of my personality. I enjoyed the music and let my body groove to the beats.

When you groove, you have to move your hips. I tried to channel that energy into walking. I knew I had to be able to move my hips to stand up and walk. I let the rhythm guide my hips, but instead of swaying, I tried to walk.

Music was essential to my soul, but I had gone through a tough time that stopped me from reforming my connection to music. After the incident, I felt something again whenever I listened to music. Whenever that person played music, it allowed my mind to rekindle the connection. It was relaxing and helped me calm my nerves and focus on making more movements.

I was finally letting myself adapt to the new changes. Yes, it was not going to be the same as before, but it was a mountain I had to climb. There was no point in turning back now. If God could make it possible for me to move my finger, He could also help me make more movements if I kept believing in Him.

Someone who became a pivotal part of my progress was my massage therapist, Patricia Dillard. She was a skilled professional with many years of experience in the field. She was one of the people who believed that I was going to walk again.

Patricia didn't leave any stone unturned to ensure I was getting everything I needed. It wasn't operations that were going to help me out. I had undergone many of them. Doctors had done all kinds of experiments on me which proved to be useless.

I needed serious attention from people who could help me move. The doctors never believed that I would recover, so they never tried any other method to help me get back on my feet again.

I could count on Patricia to show up when I needed her. I called her to tell her I was paralyzed from the neck down and needed her help. She didn't think for a second and rushed to see me immediately. She drove for an hour to see me. It meant a great deal to me as so many people had abandoned me.

I no longer had any expectations from people around me, but she was the person who made me believe that I could trust people again. Her assistance went a long way. Patricia used to perform acupuncture on me, which would give me relief. She had a lot of tricks up her sleeve as she had been in the field for a while. Patricia never saw me as an impossible case. She believed in her methods and me as well. I believe she tried to make every possible effort to improve my mobility.

My case wasn't a simple one. It had many complexities and layers to it. There was no explanation as to why I had gotten paralyzed as I was a very healthy person before. So yes, she had to start from scratch and figure out what could be done that would help me.

My condition still appeared hopeless to a lot of people. It didn't matter to them that I had managed to move my finger. They only saw someone who couldn't get up from his bed. As a result, I was refused physical therapy due to my debilitating state.

It was when Melanie, the director of social services I had become friends with suggested I should continue physical therapy on my own. She knew that I was constantly trying to make progress. I didn't know if I could handle it on my own, but she believed in me and motivated me to take things into my hands.

That motivation was all I needed. I had people standing behind me, supporting me through my struggles, and it renewed my faith in humanity and God. I knew that after the incident of witnessing Jesus' spirit present in the room with me, anything was possible if I simply kept believing.

I was determined to improve my condition and I wasn't backing down. No one could halt my progress now as I knew that God, Himself had my back, and He wanted me to succeed.

The staff assigned to me kept motivating me and making me believe I could do it. They had witnessed the miracle I had experienced. I had arrived at the nursing home as someone who had no hope of getting better, and now I was able to move my hand.

I started taking matters into my own hands and finally resumed physical therapy independently. I didn't care that the doctors thought my condition was so bad that it couldn't be helped through physical therapy anymore.

I had seen the worse. I saw my body giving up and witnessed people I believed blindly in, giving up on me. I realized that all I had was myself, and if my prayers could make such a big difference, then the sky was the limit for me.

There was nothing left for me to lose anymore. I had been at my lowest and had seen people abandon me. If there was anything I knew, it was that it couldn't get worse than this. I had seen everything now. I saw doctors telling me that I would never be able to move, and they left me to die.

I had been left to fend for myself. It was very clear to me that I couldn't rely on anyone for anything. I had to erase all the expectations I had from the people around me. It was time for me to let go of the beliefs I held close to me.

It is ironic how much you can learn when you're put through trials and tribulations. You can spend your entire life struggling to find the meaning of life and explore the truth, yet only a single blow will force you to realize the truth of the world.

Sure, I was breathing, but it wasn't enough. The torture I was going through was intolerable. Every now and then people I trusted abandoned me. It started becoming a pattern, and I started to recognize it.

I knew it was time to start over again. I still had a lot to lose. I wasn't ready to let go of life. I needed a strong faith in life and a higher power to start my journey to recovery.

My faith in people had been shattered, and there was no way I could restore that trust. So it was when God took charge of my destiny and decided to turn around my fate.

But I also witnessed God's power, and that experience was far stronger than the many hopeless situations I had witnessed. His mercy and love worked like medicine for me.

All those prayers I made to God during the lonely nights in the nursing hospital weren't useless. I had been sharing my pain with God because I knew that if someone wasn't going to leave me, it was Him.

During the time I was paralyzed, I came up with something called mental yoga. I couldn't practice physical yoga as I wasn't physically able to do that. It hit me that I could still do yoga but through my mind.

The purpose of yoga is to release tension from the body and help loosen muscles. It was the same with the mind. My mind was working perfectly fine, and I was hopeful now. I wanted to increase my focus on physical improvement.

I began practicing meditation as it had a calming effect on my mind. I would close my eyes and try not to think about anything. I knew that I had to detach all the negativity from myself. I needed to strengthen my mind if I wanted to make progress.

I trained my mind to stay still and not let any movement or disruption take away my focus. People usually expected patients like me to sulk in bed, but I wasn't doing that anymore. No one saw it coming, but I had faith in myself. I spent a lot of time practicing meditation.

Once I figured that mental yoga was helping me focus on my physical improvement, I started investing more time in practicing it. I became more aware of myself and my surroundings as I went deeper into the art of meditation.

I shifted my focus to breathing and realized that I had been restraining myself from relaxation. I have had so many panic attacks, affecting my mental peace. I was all over the place before I started practicing meditation. Mental yoga helped me find my center and focus on what was important.

Once I had my focus, I began trying to move my feet. Patricia was also helping me improve my mobility. I would try to move my toes, and once I saw that it was working, I tried to move other parts of my body.

I wasn't doing everything on my own. An entire team was helping me with every step I took. Whether I was trying to move my arms or feet, the nurse, my trainer, and Patricia were encouraging me throughout the process. The nurse would encourage me with my physical therapy, and my trainer would help me try to make small movements.

We were taking one step at a time. I didn't exert myself because I knew I needed to balance practice and rest. I had to recover the energy that I was investing in physical therapy. I went slowly at it and gave my body time to adapt to the changes.

Whenever I was meditating, I would picture myself walking again. Even though I imagined the situation, it was comforting and gave me hope. I knew what I wanted, and I was willing to work hard for it.

I started making major progress as I could sit on my own now, which was something no one had expected from me. It felt like I had climbed a mountain because I had worked so hard for it.

Gradually, I also started moving my feet, and finally, I could stand up again. When my feet touched the ground, I felt a comfort so great that nothing could compare to it. Even though I got up on my feet, I still needed a walker to walk. It was helpful as it supported my weight, and of course, there were people around me to make sure I didn't fall.

I was happy that I was making progress, but I knew it was only the beginning. I had a long way to go. I required a walker to stand on my feet, but I firmly believed that I was destined to see a day when I would be able to walk on my own once again.

God had taken me this far, and He was going to help me walk on my feet without any support as well. My faith grew stronger. I thanked God every day when I unlocked a new level of progress. If it weren't for Him, I wouldn't have been able to lift my finger.

My connection with God only became deeper during that time. I promised Him that I would tell everyone what He had managed to do if He made me walk again, and I remembered my promise.

The restroom was fifteen steps away, but I was extremely weak at that point, and those fifteen steps seemed like a million. There were several instances where I would try to walk to the restroom with the help of a walker and burst my head open after crashing into something.

I still had a huge leap to take: Walking without any support. It was an extremely difficult challenge, but I knew I had come this far, so I could succeed if I kept believing in God.

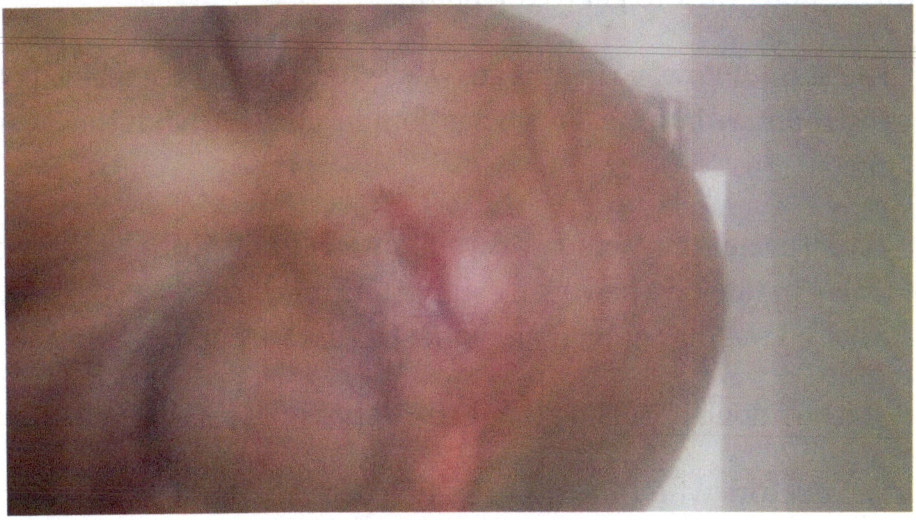

*When I ended up hurting my head as I tried to use the walker for the first time*

Every time I took a step, the staff cheered for me. They would make noise and hype me as I tried to walk. It felt like I was on a mission and had an army of support behind me that was cheering on me.

Then one day, I finally did it. Oh God, I was so happy I could die. Finally, I walked to the washroom myself. It was the day my life changed but for the better this time.

I could walk again.

It felt like I had hit the lottery.

It had taken me an entire year to take the leap of faith. A year that was met with a constant struggle for survival. I didn't just wake up one day and started walking. It had taken a long time of struggle and effort to get to the point.

The staff of Poway Healthcare was astonished to see me walk to the restroom with the walker. They couldn't believe what they were seeing.

"You're the first person to walk out of this facility," the staff told me. That facility had been established for the last 60 years, and it surprised me that only I had managed to walk out of that place.

God had done it. He had made the impossible come true.

The doctors who told me I could never walk were going to see me walk again.

# Chapter 8: Passing Challenges

The walk to the restroom was the first step of my journey to recovery. I had started to take baby steps toward healing and succeeded at it. Every day I would get up with my faith firm and unshakable, trying to make progress in whatever way I could.

I dreamed of finally being able to walk out of the facility. The hope ignited a spark in me. Shortly before, I was heartbroken and left in isolation, and here I was, getting cheered on by the facility staff, encouraging me with every step I took.

The day wasn't far when I was going to be able to walk without a walker. I could feel it in my bones. The holy intervention had completely transformed the way I looked at life. I didn't feel that I was alone. God was with me, and he had sent all these people to help in my journey of healing.

People who possessed virtue and kindness soon filled the void left by the ones I had expectations from. My entire world was shaken and broken down before God gave me the courage to look at life from a different perspective.

I had to reconsider every lesson I had learned in my life. This was a new chapter in my life. A year and a half earlier, I thought I had reached the end of the road, and there was no hope left for me now. I had been losing faith in any possibility of recovery. My misery remained to haunt me until I surrendered to God and left it in his hands to put an end to the agony I was put through.

As I continued on the path of recovery, I found people who also wanted to help me by pushing me to do better every day. Each day for me was the equivalent of fighting on the battlefield. I had to get up every morning and promise to try to make progress.

I had already managed to walk up to the restroom with a walker and initiated the healing process, but now I had more to do. Melanie, director of social services at Poway Healthcare Center who had been generous to me with assistance throughout the process now had a new challenge for me. She wanted me to walk from my room to her office.

"Hey, I want you to walk to my office," Melanie had given me the challenge.

Melanie's office was at a great distance from my room. It was on the other side of the building. It was not similar to walking to the restroom. I had to climb fifty steps to walk to the office which was a big deal for me. It was a big challenge for me which almost seemed impossible. I had just started to walk on my feet. My legs were still very weak from the paralysis. I had to pull up all my strength to take the first step, and I couldn't even imagine what I had to do so I could manage to walk up to her office.

My legs were still fragile and were already pushing beyond their limits when I started getting up and walking to the restroom. I would sway and struggle to find my ground while walking. I used to be afraid whenever I would get up. I didn't know if my legs were going to make it. I had to take a risk every time. I knew very well that I could fall anytime, given my condition, but I had to keep faith in God.

There was no way I was going to sit back now. I knew the challenge had to be completed. So, I made it my goal to make it to that office. It wasn't very far, but it felt like it was at a great distance. She kept pushing me because she believed in me. It was incredible how these people I had met just a year and a half ago now believed in me more than the ones who were supposed to.

I got up one day and began walking toward the staff member's office which belonged to Melanie, director of social services. I could feel the ground beneath my feet and the people around me. They were cheering on me. I had my mind fixed at the office. I kept thinking about how rewarding the moment would be once I reached the office.

Finally, I made it.

I reached the office. I had achieved yet another mark. I knew God was behind me when I walked the ground, and he had my back. He was the only one who had made it possible for me to come this far.

As I walked the hallway of Poway Healthcare Center, I reflected on my experience with the doctors who had told me that I was going to die. I thought about how certain they seemed while declaring I had no hope.

The images flashed in front of my eyes. I was in that dreaded hospital ward where doctors would visit. They would mock me and tell me that I wouldn't make it.

What were simply words to those unkind people felt like a death sentence to me. I was immobile. I was lying in a bed and couldn't move my body. I didn't need to hear that I was going to die. The time I spent there was awful and continued to give me nightmares.

People in the hospital would pity me and think I wasn't going to make it, yet here I was, alive and able to walk on my feet. They might have believed nothing else left for me, but they were wrong.

I was going to prove those doctors wrong. I had promised myself that I would defy everyone's expectations and continue fighting. It didn't matter to me that they didn't believe I was going to walk again. What mattered to me was what God wanted from me.

God gave me the courage to walk once again. He enabled me to prove those people wrong who gave up on me. I was left to die, yet I was living and getting better every day.

My recovery journey was a long process. I had to be patient. It was easy to lose hope during this turbulent time. Every time I fumbled and fell, disappointment would creep up on me again. I would feel discouraged, fearing that I would be unable to make it.

Some days I would manage to unlock another phase of my recovery, and some days, I wouldn't be able to do anything. My growth was not consistent. Not every day would I wake up feeling like I was going to conquer the world.

I had to tell myself that there was no option except to push myself to my limits. I had to bear witness to the cruelty of the people who were supposed to be there for me. It wasn't easy to recover from the trauma they had caused me on top of the paralysis.

The staff of Poway Healthcare Center became my family. They prayed for my recovery, pushed me to do better, and encouraged me. I was not allowed to believe that I couldn't make it. Instead, they ensured that I believed in my strength.

One day, I was informed that some of my friends were going to visit me. I thought they had finally decided to try to check up on me. I was alone in that place, so it was a big deal for me that my friends were coming to see me.

I knew they had seen a very different Rob. I used to be extremely fit and active. I had been known for my lifestyle, and people admired me for my physical strength. My friends were going to witness a very different version of me. I was no longer the same person who could go run around and have fun. I was a sick person who was stuck in his bed.

The thought of my friends finding me in a helpless state haunted me. But nonetheless, I was excited to see them once again. Solitude had been creeping up on me. I didn't have a lot of people to talk to me, which was a strange experience for me.

I had always been surrounded by lively company and never lacked friends. Yet everything was different here. I was lying on a single bed all day long, followed by an even longer night.

What followed during my friends' visit shocked me to my core. I had been expecting to see the cheerful faces who would try to lift me up but what I saw were inquiring faces who were simply there to make sure that I was paralyzed.

I couldn't grasp the reality. I thought my friends were there to see how I was, but I was wrong. They had no intention of checking up on me or trying to look after me. They just wanted to see if I was actually sick or not.

My misery had been turned into a spectacle. Here I was, fighting for my life every day, yet my friends still found it hard to believe that I had been paralyzed.

The little flicker of hope I had when I heard about them coming to see me died soon. I had lost not just the support of my family but my friends as well.

All I wanted for my friends was to be there for me when I needed them. Instead, I kept thinking about how they would be devastated when they found out about my situation. I was in a terrible state, and my torment was undeniable.

I looked at my friends. They were standing in the same room. They were the same people I had always helped and looked after. I couldn't figure out how the situation changed.

How can someone be so indifferent to someone's misery? I guess I will never know. It was not easy for me to process the trauma. I had been hurt once again by the people I loved.

My faith in people had been shattered, and there was no way I could restore that trust. It was when God took charge of my destiny and decided to turn around my fate.

When I had no one, I turned to Him and sought His guidance. I knew He was there, and He was listening to me. We often feel that we're the only people suffering in the world, yet there is someone out there who never ceases to look after us.

It is God.

God has done the miracle of turning strangers into my support system. I had pleaded with Him for a long time. I yearned for support and love. I had cried countless nights, wondering what I had done to receive my pain.

As my prayers got longer, my body became stronger. Finally, I started getting rid of the fear deeply engraved in me. I knew that if I put my mind to achieving something, no one would stop me.

I had witnessed the worse and couldn't think of anything that could crush my soul anymore. The damage had been done. People had given up on me. They thought I was going to die. I had nothing to be afraid of anymore.

There was only one-way one, and it was the way forward. I didn't plan to look back. I wanted to keep my mind focused on my physical and mental growth.

The prayers strengthened my faith in life, and my body strengthened against the restraint it had faced. My spiritual and physical journey went hand in hand. One couldn't survive without the other.

Every tool I was using to make progress was showing results now. I couldn't manage to walk up to the restroom that was merely fifteen steps away, and here I was, walking to the nurse's office. I knew in my heart that God had worked his miracle, and it was time for me to prove that I was worthy of his blessings.

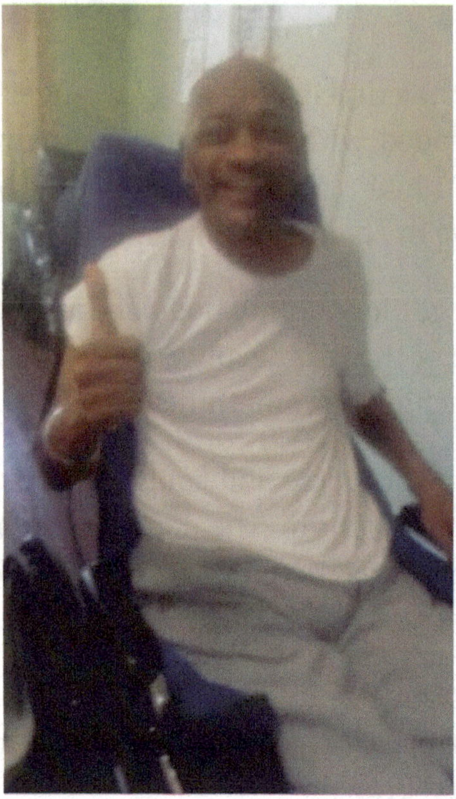

*When I weighed 161 pounds*

The day I had the conversation with God remained engraved in my mind. He had asked me if I believed He could heal me. I believed in His power blindly. I knew He was the only one who could make the impossible possible.

If I didn't have the hope that I could survive, I couldn't have come this far. It was my resilient nature that had brought me here.

Anyone in my position would have thought their life was over, and I thought that as well. It was hard not to think otherwise.

We often lose hope in the face of the daily difficulties we face. I would lie in bed thinking about what I would do if it weren't for my faith in God and myself.

When all doors were closed on me, God carved a new path for me. I had no one to rely on, so He became my sole support. People were not aware of the power of miracles, but God was about to show them how wrong they were.

My first step on the ground was the moment my soul came back to my body. God had enabled me to believe in myself, and I no longer had any doubts in my mind.

The goal was clear. I had to heal myself. There was still a lot of work that needed to be done. It took great strength to wake up every day and work on faith, but I did it. I proved to those people out there that I could survive on my own.

They thought I was alone, but God had been with me. He took me out of the darkest place and made me walk again. My belief had been restored. At that point, I knew that if God was capable of making a miracle like that come true, then anything was possible.

# Chapter 9: Miracles Are Real

If anyone had told me that my life was going to be turned upside down and that I would then find the courage to rise again, I wouldn't have believed them. Even in my wildest dreams, I never imagined that I would end up confined to a hospital bed, deprived of any physical movement, just to be revived by God.

Reflecting on what I was put through, I cannot fathom how I managed to have courage throughout my trial. I was hopeless, tired, and alone. Yet God held my hands through my darkest times and taught me to keep my faith strong.

I was told by the doctors that I was never going to walk again, but God proved them wrong. I gathered the strength and the courage to get up and prove to those doctors that I could walk.

My first steps after the long-term paralysis reaffirmed my belief in God. If it wasn't for my faith and hope, I wouldn't have been able to make it. There is no doubt that God was behind me every time I tried to move, sit, or walk. He supported, encouraged, and pushed me to bring out my best.

As soon as I put my feet on the ground and felt the strength in my legs, I knew that I would walk. I recovered by stepping on the path of faith and hope, and I'd tell everyone to do the same.

I made it when everyone told me I was not going to. I was alive and fighting. There was no way I was going to bow down to the circumstances. No force could have held me back from achieving what I wanted.

The strength in me was a blessing from God. He decided to have mercy on me, and it was His blessing that allowed me to believe in myself. I walked like I was walking for the first time. I didn't care if I was going to make it or not since every fear had left my body when God gave me back my hope.

I was no longer alone because I knew God was with me. When I walked for the first time, I kept thinking about how everyone thought I would never walk again. I often wondered where my life would be if it wasn't for my stubbornness to survive.

It is easy to lose yourself when life throws its worst challenges at you. Life might seem like it's never going to get better, but my story should teach you that there is always hope as long as you believe in yourself.

Every force in the universe can ally against you and try to take you down, but only you can change your fate, just like I had the strength to alter my life and prove everyone wrong.

Not too long ago, I found myself in a dark pit. I couldn't find a way out. I thought I would be stuck there forever or die there. Yet, I decided not to lose hope. I turned to faith in the absence of support and made it the source of my strength.

Soon, I began to push myself. I was not going to give up; that is exactly what I emphasize in my life now. I don't want anyone to suffer alone as I did. I decided to become people's strength and began thinking about how to achieve my purpose.

As someone who witnessed agony and betrayal, I understand what it feels like not to have anyone by your side when you need them the most. I understand that life can knock you down, and you might end up hopeless. That's the reason I decided to help people see hope beyond despair.

It's not wrong to feel hopeless or depressed. It's a natural reaction to the situation you might be facing. It's a constant struggle that you will have to face. Remember that giving in is not an option, and you must gather all your courage to rise again.

No one can help you if you cannot help yourself, and that's something I have learned from my experience. It wasn't until I stood up for myself that things started to work out. I would have never made it if I had remained in the same bed and continued staying hopeless.

My first step to recovery was faith. After all, my faith was going to carve out a path for me. I started to see things clearly when I saw that God could do anything. I didn't have the tools to achieve my goals, but I had my strength, and it would take me a long way.

If it wasn't for that trip to Fresno, my life would have been completely different. One moment, I was living an entirely regular life; the next, I was confined to a bed, told I'd never walk again, and left all alone. When I went to visit my sister in Fresno, I had no idea what was awaiting me; all I wanted was to see her and have a good time. I was unsuspecting of what had been cooking against me behind my back.

I trusted Debra despite the friction in our relationship. After all, she was my sister, and family mattered the world to me. I had never been the person who took his family for granted. I was someone who always contributed to the harmony of the family.

I had already lost my parents and didn't want to lose anyone else. My mother was one strong woman who believed in keeping the family together. She was the glue that held us all in place. I didn't want to be disrespectful to her memory, so I stepped up as the binding factor once she was gone.

A lot of people tend to take the concept of family for granted, but I didn't. I knew that we all needed each other. Life is long, and you need all the support you can get. I had never been bitter as I didn't believe in keeping grudges.

In the end, I believed I wouldn't be harmed as long as I didn't harm anyone. I wanted to keep my conscience clear. I wasn't someone who looked for problems, so I tried my best to keep a cordial equation with everyone around me.

Little did I know that all my beliefs would get shattered before I could finally build myself again. I trusted Debra because she was my blood and my sister. Alas, I couldn't even trust her with life.

The last thing I expected from Debra was to inflict harm on me. She knew that I was a lively and active person. My physical health was one of the most important aspects of my life. People could not tell my age when they saw how active I was.

My own sister tried to snatch away my life from me. She was the person who became the reason for my inability to operate like a normal person.

I was healthy when I walked into Debra's house, yet I left it paralyzed, unable to move, and on a stretcher. A friendly visit to my sister's house ended up costing me my entire life.

My whole life flashed before me as I was forcefully taken to a hospital that I didn't want to go to in the first place. Not only did my sister try to harm me, but she also tried to make sure that I didn't have any way of escaping the torture she had premeditated for me.

It was the day when I realized that I couldn't trust my own blood. What started as a sharp pain ended up paralyzing my entire body.

The man known for his fitness could no longer move. He couldn't get up from his bed. He couldn't eat. He couldn't even walk to the washroom.

I couldn't recognize myself when I was kept hostage in the ghetto hospital in Fresno. I kept hoping that someone would come to my rescue. After all, I had spent my life caring for and helping people.

Yet, despite my hopes, it soon became apparent that I was alone in my battle. I wasn't going to get a savior. People I loved and cared for had chosen their stance, and I had to choose mine. I had to be my own savior. I was the sole warrior in my battle, and losing meant dying.

It's ironic that we as humans spend our entire life building relationships with others. We rely on these people and expect them to help us when we are in need. We do everything in our power to save these relationships when we know God has told us to seek Him when facing obstacles.

Since we are mere mortals, we tend to gravitate toward the colossal appeal of other mortals. We keep forgetting that humans cannot risk their own interests for the well-being of others.

I had to learn the hard way that I couldn't count on mortals. They would never rescue me because they didn't owe me anything. They thought that my life was over. I believed that as well. There was nothing left for me. I had turned into a vegetable that could be cut open anytime since I wasn't given the liberty to choose my fate.

When I had lost all hope, and my spirit had been snatched away from me, I found solace in faith. As soon as I started strengthening my faith, I began sensing a purpose in my life.

After long prayers and pleas to God, He finally answered me. He gave me another chance at life; I had to give it my everything this time.

The first time I walked, I felt like I was alive again. That was when I let go of all my beliefs associated with mortals. I learned that I had to start relying on God instead of people who had abandoned me when I needed them the most.

After my battle against death, I learned that my fate never lay in the hands of the people who believed I would die. Only God could decide my fate, and He blessed me with the strength to fight against all odds.

I fought for a long time. I wasn't alone in that battle because God was always with me. He was there when I didn't have anyone else. He gave me strength when I had lost everything.

After going through a near-death experience, I have concluded that faith keeps us alive when we have lost everything. We need to get rid of the expectations we associate with mortals. We need to change our direction and seek God's guidance instead of mortals'. He is the one who gave us life and is the only one with the right to take it away.

*The Will to Live: Rob Halliburton Testimony 2020 (Based on a True Story)* is available on YouTube and chronicles my experience of beating the odds.

https://www.youtube.com/watch?v=h_8a04CvdUM

*"Hello, Rob,*

*This is Joshua Labiano from the rock church. I prayed for you last afternoon at the altar. I wanted to let you know that your story is an inspiring and heartwarming video. God is going to use your testimony in many good ways to reach others in salvation. I wanted to reach out and get to know you.*

*I watched your second video. I see that you are in sales. Looking forward to hearing from you and chatting with you.*

*Respectfully Submitted,*

*Joshua Florentino San Nicolas Labiano."*

*"Morning Rob!*

*Just wanted you to know that I am very fortunate to be able to meet with you and assist you. You may have a huge impact! You have been a great positive motivator for our community. Your video is very inspirational!*

*Thanks for serving and inspiring people, which we need big time now than ever!*

*Thank you!*

*Rika Ray."*

SHARP Grossmont Hospital

Ecrobhalliburton@gmail.com

Made in the USA
Coppell, TX
14 April 2026

75566765R00059